FIRST CAMPING TRIP

WRITTEN AND ILLUSTRATED BY
C. B. COLBY

COWARD-McCANN, Inc. 72543 NEW YORK

COVER PHOTO BY C. EVERETT GARVEY

Fifth Impression

COPYRIGHT, 1955, BY C. B. COLBY

Manufactured in the United States of America

FOREWORD

The first camping trip will be a wonderful adventure no matter what the age of the camper, but to the boy or girl who has not before spent a night in the woods, it will be a thrilling experience, full of new sights, sounds, smells and thrills.

The thrills are part of the fun of camping. Every night-sound of rustling leaves will be "a bear" at least, instead of a shy woodmouse, raccoon, or deer attracted by your campfire. Every snapping twig will at once become something big and mysterious, and every shooting star a thrill to gasp at and remember. It's almost a shame to go to sleep that first night!

Only a very small part of camping lore and advice can be packed into one small book. Years of experience cannot be told or illustrated in a few pages, but here are some tips, some "do's" and "don't's," and some friendly advice to help you look forward to, plan, and carry out that First Camping Trip. May you learn from experience much more than you could find in a library of such books, and may every lesson be fun, and every classroom deep in the back-country woods.

May every camping trip be full of adventure, good fun, good stories, and good nights as well as days. May you see your full share of shooting stars and hear your share of night noises, and may you sleep warm and deeply at last when the fire burns low, and for the umteenth time you've all said "good night," only to think of one thing more to talk about.

My sincere thanks to friend Harry Harchar, Editor of *Boys' Life* magazine, and F. C. Smith and Bill Hillcourt of the Boy Scouts of America, for their suggestions and help with this book, and to the many guys with whom I have shared campfires in distant places. They too, unknowingly, were helping me collect material for this book, and I now pass along to you from those campfires these pages of help so that yours may be a pleasant and thrilling First Camping Trip!

C. B. COLBY

CONTENTS

PICKING A CAMP SITE

If you are to camp only a night or so, a tent or sleeping bag will do as well as a lean-to and you will not waste the wood for its construction and thatching.

THINGS TO LOOK FOR WHEN PICKING A CAMP SITE

A—FRESH WATER NEARBY FOR DRINKING, COOKING AND FIRE
B—LEVEL DRY GROUND FREE FROM ROCKS AND HOLES
C—GOOD DRAINAGE AWAY FROM WHERE SHELTER WILL BE
D—STONES FOR FIREPLACE AND OTHER CAMP USES
E—DRY FIREWOOD IN ABUNDANCE FAIRLY CLOSE TO SITE
F—WOOD FOR BUILDING LEAN-TO AND CAMP FURNITURE
G—EVERGREENS FOR THATCHING LEAN-TO AND FILLING BEDS

IF YOU PLAN TO USE TENTS OR SLEEPING BAGS
RATHER THAN BUILD A LEAN-TO, YOU CAN GET ALONG
WITHOUT EITHER ITEM "F" OR "G" IN ABOVE LIST

5

THINGS NOT TO CAMP NEAR!

LARGE ANT HILLS. THESE LOOK LIKE PILES OF SAND IN THE GRASS AND HOLD THOUSANDS OF ANTS TO BOTHER OR BITE

HORNETS' NESTS OF ANY KIND OR SIZE. DO NOT DISTURB IN ANY WAY AS THEIR STINGS CAN BE FATAL

A

B

C

A—POISON OAK; B—POISON IVY; C—POISON SUMAC. ANY OF THESE CAN SPOIL YOUR CAMPING TRIP. THEIR POISON CAUSES SKIN REDNESS, RASH, BLISTERS AND VIOLENT ITCHING. KEEP AWAY FROM ANY SUSPICIOUS PLANTS RESEMBLING ANY OF THESE BUT IF YOU CONTACT THEM, WASH THOROUGHLY WITH HEAVY SOAPSUDS

STAGNANT WATER OR SWAMPS. THEY HARBOR SWARMS OF INSECTS

USING A HAND AX

ALWAYS CHOP WOOD ON WOOD, OR UPON HARD GROUND, NEVER ON ROCK. A DULL AX IS DANGEROUS. KEEP IT SHARP TO PREVENT SLIPPING DANGER

WHEN SPLITTING KINDLING WOOD HOLD AX AND WOOD TOGETHER AND HIT UPON LOG TOGETHER AS ONE UNIT

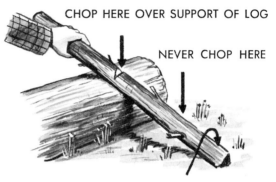

CHOP HERE OVER SUPPORT OF LOG

NEVER CHOP HERE

SOME WOODSMEN PREFER ANOTHER LOG PLACED OVER THIS FREE END OF STICK

CUT ONCE HERE AND THEN CUT ON TOP AND BREAK OFF

In cutting dead limbs for firewood cut close to trunk, never away from it, where branch is springy and may cause ax to bounce dangerously with each blow.

Trimming branches from felled trees is done by cutting from the underside of branch, never from the crotch side. Work from butt of log up along length to top.

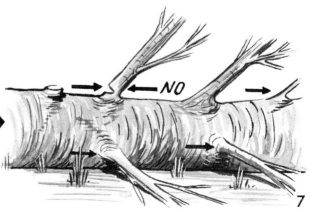

NO

7

USING A LONG-HANDLED AX

PICKING UP AND UPSWING. RAISE AX WITH ONE HAND NEAR HEAD. BE SURE THERE IS NOTHING OVERHEAD TO STRIKE WITH RAISED AX

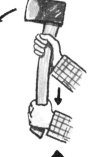

BLOW. UPPER HAND SLIDES DOWN HANDLE AS AX COMES DOWN. STAND WITH FEET APART AND ON SAFELY SECURE FOOTING BELOW

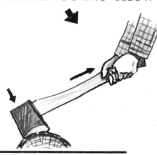

TOP OF SWING

A

To tighten loosened ax head, pound upon grip end of handle, not upon head of ax. Cut off piece "A" for better spot to pound. Add another wedge beside old one, or grease head and soak to swell handle tighter.

Safe carry for ax is over shoulder with blade down, or by handle with hand close to head and edge down. Never carry with blade toward body!

8

CUTTING TIMBER

WIND →
FALL →

FALL WIND

NEVER STAND BE-HIND TREE AS IT IS FALLING!

When you are cutting standing timber determine which way, if any, it is leaning. Always fall a tree in direction of lean or down wind. Make a notch "A—B" beyond center and then notch "C—D" a bit above it. Tree falls toward cut "A—B." Stand clear of falling tree.

When splitting small logs, place against far side of log to protect legs from ax blade, should you miss or ax slip. Keep feet well apart.

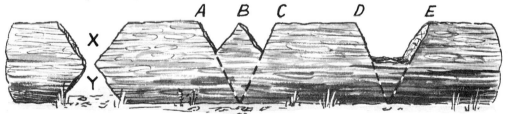

To cut a log, start two cuts, "A—B" and "B—C" and cut them both until the center piece can be knocked out. Then continue to bottom of log as at "D—E." If log can be rolled, make two cuts to center as at "X" and "Y" and chop through. This is particularly good if cutting through as at "D—E" ax strikes rock.

9

USE AND CARE OF HUNTING KNIFE

Always cut away from you, never toward any part of your body. Never use a knife as a hammer or screwdriver. When not in use keep in its sheath or where it cannot cut you or be stepped upon.

MAKING A FIRE STICK TO START FIRE WITH

WHEN REPLACING KNIFE IN SHEATH BE SURE THE BLADE FITS THE SHAPE OF THE SHEATH SO THAT THE POINT OF THE KNIFE DOES NOT CUT STITCHES AS SHOWN AT "A," IN SKETCH

HOW TO SHARPEN A KNIFE CORRECTLY

A sharp knife is a safe one, as it grips and cuts and does not slip. It also makes a clean flesh cut rather than a jagged one. Sharpen it with a whetstone by rotating the blade on the surface of the stone, holding the blade at a slight angle to the stone. Use coarse side of stone, then fine side for keen edge.

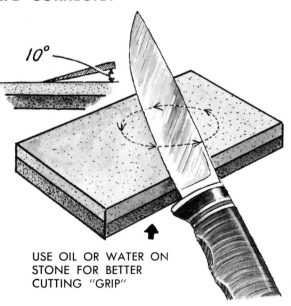

$10°$

USE OIL OR WATER ON STONE FOR BETTER CUTTING "GRIP"

10

BUILDING SHELTERS AND LEAN-TOS

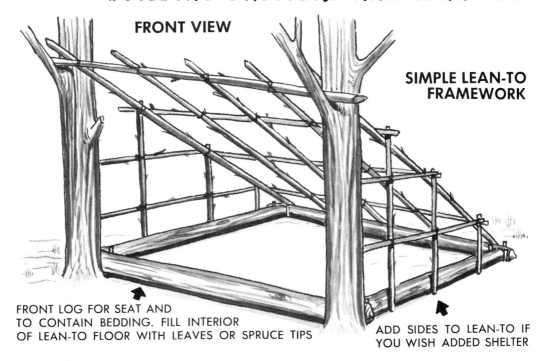

FRONT VIEW

SIMPLE LEAN-TO FRAMEWORK

FRONT LOG FOR SEAT AND
TO CONTAIN BEDDING. FILL INTERIOR
OF LEAN-TO FLOOR WITH LEAVES OR SPRUCE TIPS

ADD SIDES TO LEAN-TO IF
YOU WISH ADDED SHELTER

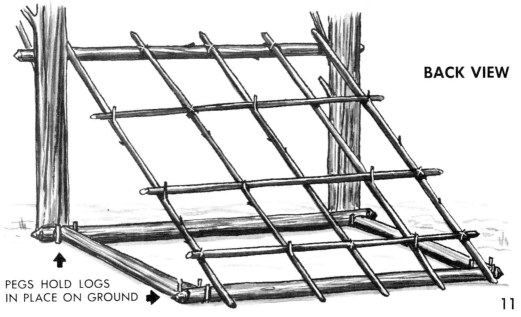

BACK VIEW

PEGS HOLD LOGS
IN PLACE ON GROUND

11

THATCHING SHELTERS

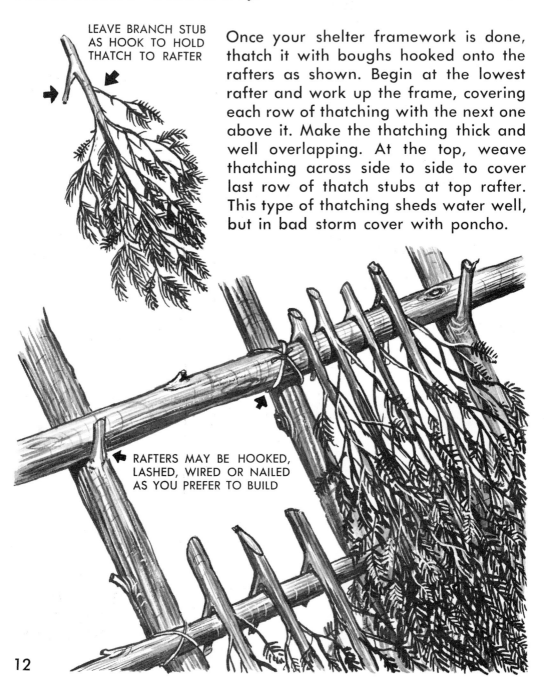

LEAVE BRANCH STUB AS HOOK TO HOLD THATCH TO RAFTER

Once your shelter framework is done, thatch it with boughs hooked onto the rafters as shown. Begin at the lowest rafter and work up the frame, covering each row of thatching with the next one above it. Make the thatching thick and well overlapping. At the top, weave thatching across side to side to cover last row of thatch stubs at top rafter. This type of thatching sheds water well, but in bad storm cover with poncho.

RAFTERS MAY BE HOOKED, LASHED, WIRED OR NAILED AS YOU PREFER TO BUILD

FIT YOUR SHELTER TO YOUR CAMP SITE *SHELTER TYPES*

Small one-man shelter made with one main pole and side walls. Rest ridge pole in tree crotch, or against ledge or boulder.

SHOVE POINTED ENDS INTO GROUND

THATCH ALL OF THESE SHELTERS WITH EVERGREEN TIPS AS SHOWN ON OPPOSITE PAGE

One-man shelter made of sapling. Remove the branches and tie tip to stout stake. Then attach side poles, add other hoops and thatch.

If no big trees are about, lean main side poles against ledge or big boulder. Fire against ledge will reflect heat into the lean-to.

RAM POINTED ENDS OF MAIN BEAMS INTO GROUND AT BACK

13

TENTS AND WAYS TO PITCH THEM

TARP TENT

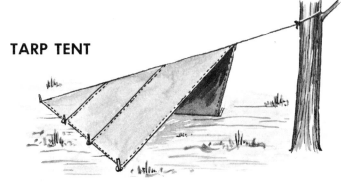

This little one-man tent is called a tarp tent and can be simply made from a poncho, old shower curtain, or tarpaulin. Just hitch one corner to a tree or upright and stake down other sides. It is small but easy to make and carry.

PUP TENT

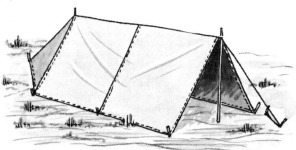

The popular pup tent will hold two men and is easy to carry and put up. Back end is closed, front open.

UMBRELLA TENT

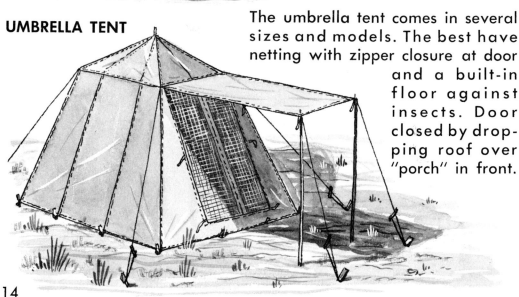

The umbrella tent comes in several sizes and models. The best have netting with zipper closure at door and a built-in floor against insects. Door closed by dropping roof over "porch" in front.

14

Wall tents come in many sizes. Sleep several men, but require more than one to erect and take down.

WALL TENT

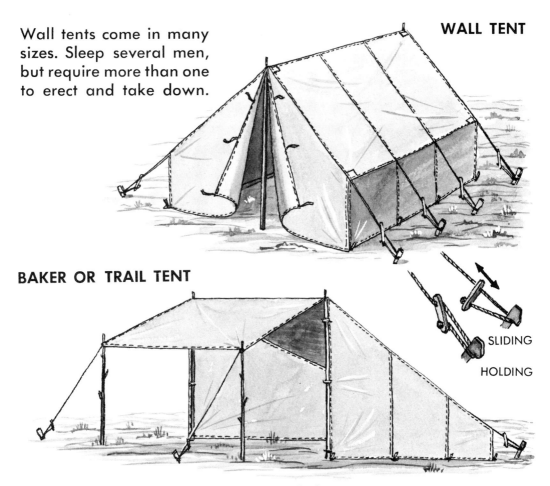

BAKER OR TRAIL TENT

SLIDING

HOLDING

Baker or Trail type has "porch roof" shelter.

Wedge tent is popular, as easy to carry and put up. May use poles.

WEDGE TENT

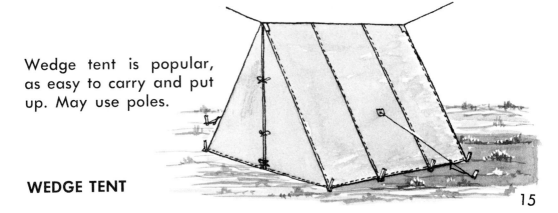

15

ALL TENTS MAY BE ERECTED SEVERAL WAYS

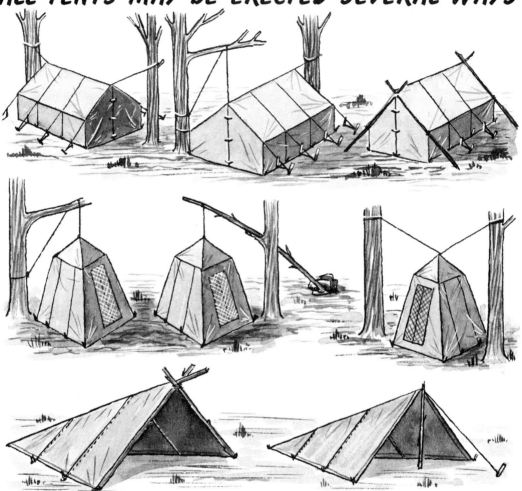

Sometimes you may not be able to pitch a tent as suggested by the usual directions that come with it. This may be from lack of poles, manpower to help, or right kind of terrain. When this happens use your ingenuity to develop some other way to erect it. Here are a few suggestions for pitching three types but these methods will also do for several other types and sizes of tents. For this reason the author suggests that you carry several feet of light rope along with you on your camping trips. It will be handy in a dozen ways.

16

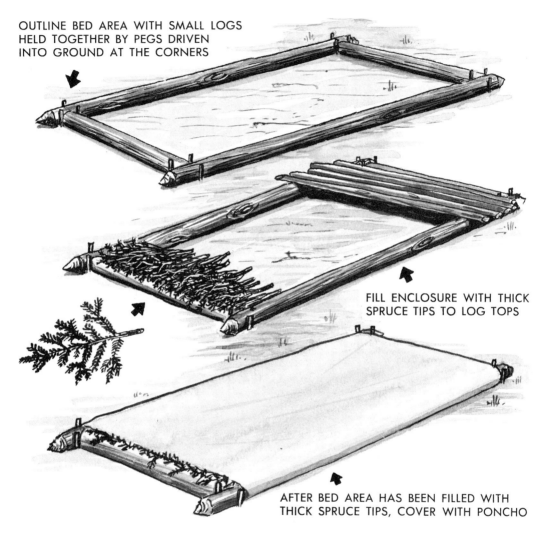

OUTLINE BED AREA WITH SMALL LOGS
HELD TOGETHER BY PEGS DRIVEN
INTO GROUND AT THE CORNERS

FILL ENCLOSURE WITH THICK
SPRUCE TIPS TO LOG TOPS

AFTER BED AREA HAS BEEN FILLED WITH
THICK SPRUCE TIPS, COVER WITH PONCHO

A well-made spruce bough bed is as comfortable as the best "store" bed ever built. Be sure you pick a level spot for your bed and clear away all stones and branches before you begin. Either fill the area within the logs deep with armfuls of evergreen tips (you can't have it too thick) or lay springy branches "A" across the base logs before you thatch with boughs. Poncho keeps out dampness under bed.

17

BLANKET SLEEPING BAGS

One kind of blanket sleeping bag is called a "mummy roll" and you simply roll yourself across the blanket taking the blanket with you, then back again covering with the poncho.

MUMMY ROLL BAG

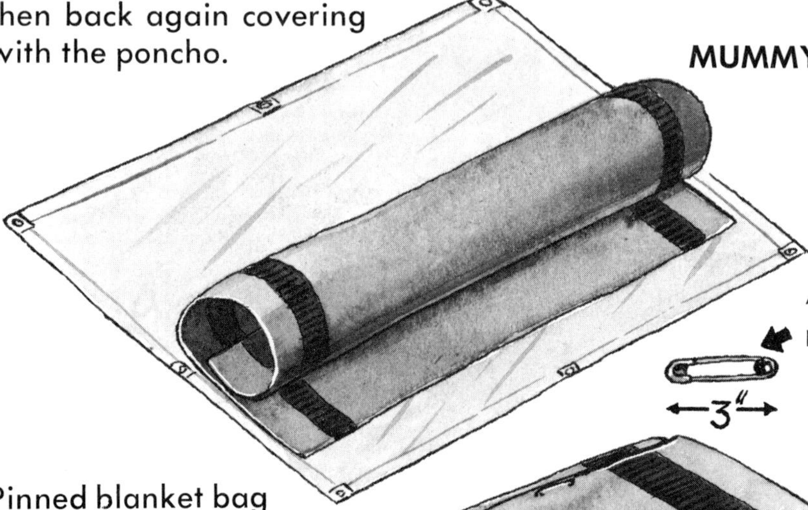

"HORSE BLANKET" PINS ARE BEST

←—3"—→

Pinned blanket bag with one or more blankets used.

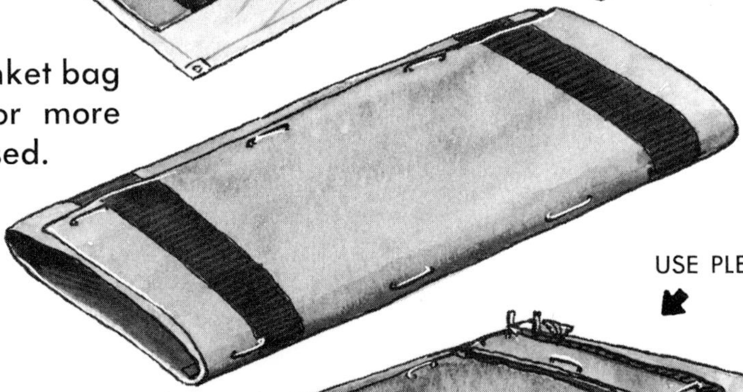

USE PLENTY OF PINS

PINNED BLANKET BAG

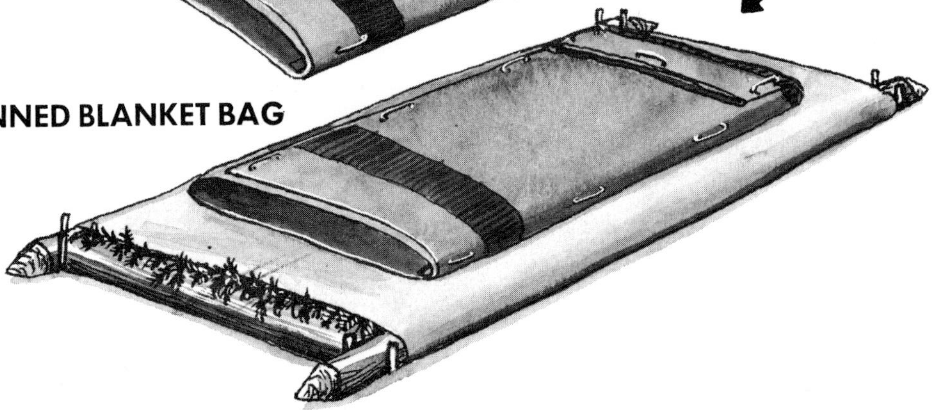

Blanket sleeping bags are satisfactory if the weather is not too cold. Be sure a poncho covers you top and bottom, and feet are pinned in.

SLEEPING BAGS

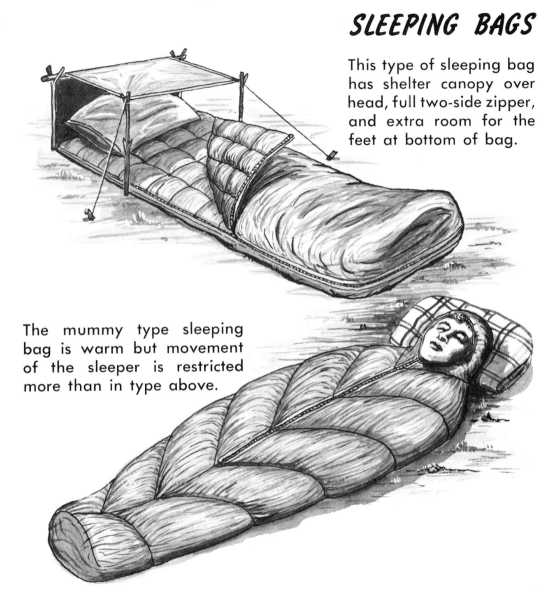

This type of sleeping bag has shelter canopy over head, full two-side zipper, and extra room for the feet at bottom of bag.

The mummy type sleeping bag is warm but movement of the sleeper is restricted more than in type above.

If you are buying a sleeping bag, get a good one. Be sure it is well made, can be opened up for airing after use, and has at least a water-repellent outside covering. They come in many models and filled with an assortment of materials: Kapok, wool, down or cotton. Talk it over with the sporting store clerk and others as to model.

19

CAMP-MADE FURNITURE

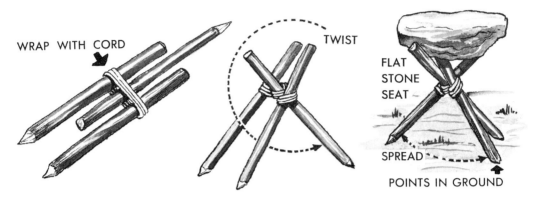

WRAP WITH CORD

TWIST

FLAT
STONE
SEAT

SPREAD

POINTS IN GROUND

Part of the fun of camping is not in seeing just how much you can get along without, but in seeing just how much "at home" you can be in the woods; inventing and constructing camp-made furniture and gadgets and conveniences out of materials at hand. Here are a few samples of simple items. Now you try and do much better!

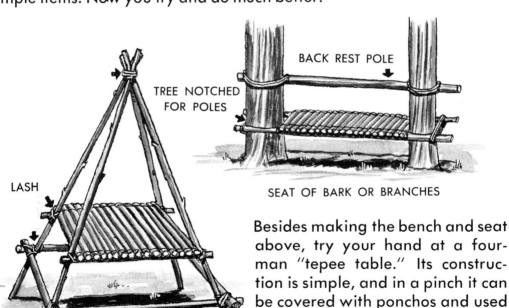

BACK REST POLE

TREE NOTCHED
FOR POLES

LASH

SEAT OF BARK OR BRANCHES

Besides making the bench and seat above, try your hand at a four-man "tepee table." Its construction is simple, and in a pinch it can be covered with ponchos and used as a shelter or to keep items up off a wet ground. It can be made in any size. Add a shelf above table.

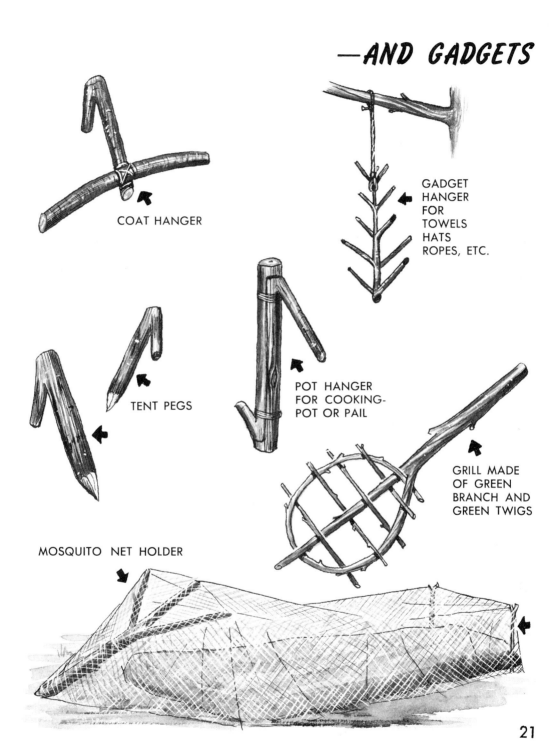

—AND GADGETS

COAT HANGER

GADGET HANGER FOR TOWELS HATS ROPES, ETC.

TENT PEGS

POT HANGER FOR COOKING-POT OR PAIL

GRILL MADE OF GREEN BRANCH AND GREEN TWIGS

MOSQUITO NET HOLDER

21

CAMP LAMPS AND LIGHTS

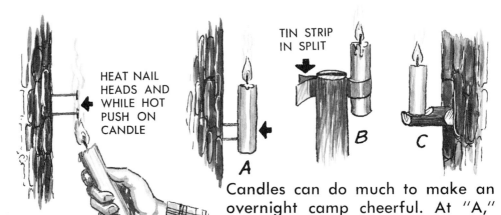

HEAT NAIL HEADS AND WHILE HOT PUSH ON CANDLE

TIN STRIP IN SPLIT

A

B

C

Candles can do much to make an overnight camp cheerful. At "A," "B," and "C" we see three simple holders. Candle "B" is held by tin can strip in split stick. Candle "C" sits on flattened peg driven into bark. When candles are burned down, snuff out for fire safety.

This tin can pole light is good for a more permanent camp. It burns well even in wind. One nail holds can to pole, other impales candle.

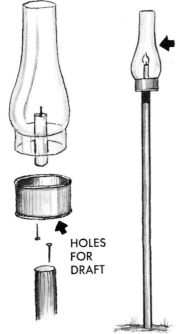

HOLES FOR DRAFT

Tin can candle light can be made from can with tin shears. The top is bent back for handle or for nailing to tree or post for outside use. Put this light on down-wind side of tree or post.

CAMP LANTERNS

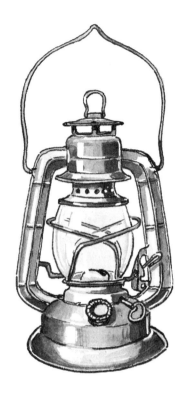

This small Dietz Comet camp lantern is light in weight (only a pound and a half filled) and is only a bit over eight inches high, yet will burn for twelve hours on one filling. It is painted a bright red for easy spotting about a camp area and the whole twelve hours of cheery light at night will cost only about two cents' worth of kerosene.

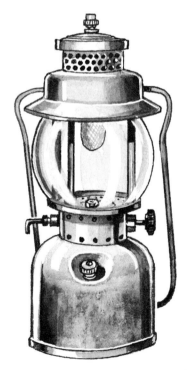

For greater camping comfort and more efficient night lighting, the Coleman gasoline lanterns have a world-wide reputation with veteran woodsmen. This safe gasoline-burning lantern holds enough fuel to burn for nearly ten hours and gives as much light as a 200-watt bulb. The gasoline mixes with air and burns in a mantle at the top of the globe. It is about a foot high.

BUILDING YOUR FIREPLACE

The most simple fireplace is a ring of rocks about the area where the fire will be built. Scrape the leaves and debris away for five feet about the fire itself, down to mineral dirt.

Building your fireplace against a cliff or ledge serves a double purpose. It is a safe place for a fire and also reflects the heat back toward any shelter you may build facing your fire. Side rocks make handy shelves for cooking utensils.

A small handy cooking fire can be made with a minimum of rocks as shown. The overlapping stones funnel the heat up to cooking pans and also serve as shelves for implements and pans. Cooking fires are better if small and concentrated in one spot. Back rock helps create draft.

24

Make a few pot holders as shown above from which to hang your pots and pails. The branch stubs are helpful for removing from the fire with a long stick as shown at right. Use stout green wood for your cooking "cranes" and do not set them too close to flames.

A simple crane for cooking can be made as shown at left. Be sure the stakes are well driven into ground and the horizontal member is stout enough for filled pail or pot. Stub on end of crane keeps pot from slipping off.

Trapper cooking fire is made between two logs with the pot or pan resting across them or across green sticks as shown. A cooking-fire pit can be made by building your fire in a shallow trench and setting the pots on green sticks placed across trench from side to side.

BUILDING THE CAMPFIRE

TINDER

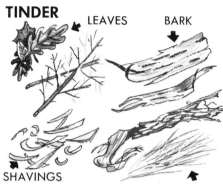

LEAVES   BARK

SHAVINGS

DRY GRASS AND PINE NEEDLES

Tinder is used to catch the match flame to start the main fire, so it should be fine in texture, absolutely dry and quick to catch fire. If you find tinder is scarce at the camp site be sure that what you do find is kept dry. Keep it in a paper bag or under cover until you use it. Soft paper tissues make good tinder, also wax paper.

KINDLING

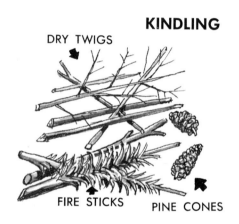

DRY TWIGS

FIRE STICKS   PINE CONES

Kindling is slightly heavier than tinder and serves to carry the first flames to the heavier fuel. If tinder is scarce use a candle to start the kindling with, especially in damp weather. Make fire sticks as shown on page 10. They catch easily and burn hotly. Also, if available, pine cones make excellent kindling, burning quickly.

FUEL

Fuel is what does the cooking and keeps the fire going all night. Split logs burn better than round ones. Use standing deadwood if possible or down timber that is dry. Keep fuel covered in wet weather or stacked closely to shed rain.

DON'T BUILD YOUR FIRE TOO BIG TO ENJOY

A nice type of cooking fire is the reflector-fire built against a back wall of logs held by stakes and braces. This throws the heat toward a shelter built in front of it and as the heat is concentrated, it is fast cooking.

Crisscross or council fire is rather large to cook over, but makes an ideal all-night fire or one to sit around at night. "Lazy logs" "A" pushed in from bed.

HOW TO PUT A CAMPFIRE SAFELY OUT

When you are leaving camp be sure your fire is dead out. Let it burn down, then sprinkle with water as at "A" (don't pour water from pail), then stir as at "B" and sprinkle again, until cool "C."

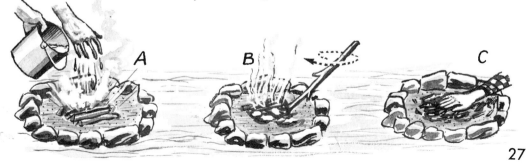

FOOD TO TAKE

CAMP MEALS SHOULD BE SIMPLE TO CARRY AND COOK

Unless you plan to be gone for several days without access to fresh food your meals should be no problem. Every camper to his own taste, but plan your meals for simplicity, nourishment and ease of cooking.

Good camp meals include steak (trim out bone and remove some of fat for lighter packing), cube steaks, bologna (can be eaten as cold cuts or fried), hot dogs, bacon. The last is staple for breakfasts as it produces fat for frying other foods. Most meats will keep for two or three days if kept in cool shade or packed in watertight containers and kept in cool water. Eggs, too, will keep in cool place.

Good canned foods include soups, stews and fruit juices. Concentrated fruit juices are good for breakfasts. (Fresh fruits spoil, bruise easily and include much waste.) Use canned condensed milk for coffee. (Boil suspicious water over 5 minutes.)

Bread is best carried in the long sandwich loaves. Do not try to bake it unless experienced as a camp cook. Carry block cheese for sandwiches along with the cold cuts. Crackers are usually more bother than worth.

Instant coffee and chocolate are good items for drinks to be made with water. Carry lump sugar to save spilling and attracting insects.

Fresh-caught fish should be cleaned, rolled in cracker crumbs (if you plan on fresh fish, carry a box with you) and fried in either bacon fat or non-spoiling Crisco. Carry several bars of hard semi-sweet chocolate for dessert, or canned fruit salad or whole canned fruit. Be sure to take salt, pepper, can and bottle openers and long-handled fork.

PACK BASKET KNAPSACK NEW TYPE PACK

Pack basket can be covered with canvas hood and is good for canned goods and "hard" items. When packing canvas packs place sweater or other soft material inside next to back.

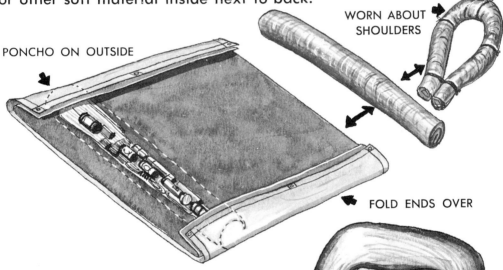

WORN ABOUT SHOULDERS

PONCHO ON OUTSIDE

FOLD ENDS OVER

If you have no pack, roll your eats and other items in your blanket and poncho and make a blanket roll to be worn about the shoulders. Fold ends over and roll tightly. Fasten with ropes or straps in several places to keep it small and tight. This can also be worn about "D"-ring pack.

"D" RING

29

CAMP COOKING

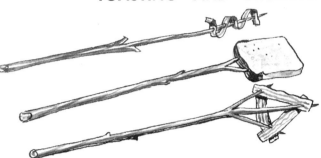

Simple cooking can be done by toasting and broiling on pointed sticks. Ideal for toast, bacon, hot dogs, etc.

One-, two-, or three-pronged sticks can be used, or make a grill such as is shown on page 21, for fish or steaks. Use green sticks for these.

Such things as bacon, steaks, hamburgers and fish can be broiled or fried in an aluminum or steel frying pan. Use butter or bacon fat to prevent sticking to pan.

PAN BROILING OR FRYING

STEWING OR BOILING

Stewing or boiling is done in either open or covered pail or pots. Eggs, stews, soups and such foods are prepared this way. The cover keeps soot and cinders out of food.

FLAT ROCK FRYING

Meat and eggs can be fried on a hot flat rock as well as in a frying pan. Use fat or grease to prevent sticking. Wash stone first.

OVENS, PLANKING AND STOVES

TIN CAN FRYING

A small and very efficient camp stove can be made from a tin can. Cut out the bottom, then a square "door" in one side at the open bottom for feeding fuel. Punch holes at back top of opposite side. Use lots of small sticks and grease top of can.

PLANKING

Peg meat or fish to a split log or board and set so that reflected heat will cook. This "planking" cooks the food slowly and well. Turn food over from time to time to cook from both sides.

BAKING IN REFLECTOR OVEN

Baking such things as canned biscuits, meat loaves, etc., can be done easily in lightweight tin reflector ovens. These are set so that heat is reflected into and onto the food from top and bottom. Set close to fire for best result.

COLEMAN CAMP STOVE

The famous Coleman camp stove is used the world over by veteran campers. Carried like a small suitcase, it opens up for cooking as shown. It burns gasoline and comes in several sizes. It can be used with folding legs to make waist-high.

72543

CARE OF FOOD

KEEPING FOOD COOL

Food and drinks may be kept cool by setting in running water in shade. Use watertight containers unless in cans, unopened. Mark canned goods on top with wax crayon or put rubber bands about labels so they will not wash away. Build wall of stones to hold in place.

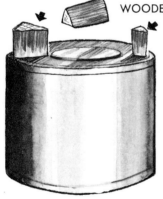

WOODEN PEGS

If canned goods are opened and not entirely used they must be sealed in some way to keep insects away. One of the best ways is to whittle wooden pegs to fit the holes and tap into place. It is better to carry several small cans of a food than one or two large ones, as only one can will be opened at a time, leaving rest sealed.

Leftovers can be sealed in metal foil or put in glass jars and sealed with wax-paper tops held with rubber bands.

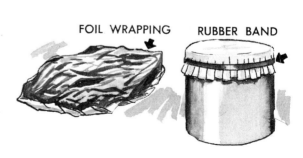

FOIL WRAPPING   RUBBER BAND

Small animals can smell food a long ways and only wait until you are asleep to see what is around your camp site for their own use. To protect your food from both animals and insects hang it to branches out of their reach. If possible hang by wire in paper bags or in your pack and cover with mosquito netting to keep out insects. Unopened food in tins is safe but all other food should be protected in this way each night.

PROTECTING FOOD AT NIGHT

NEVER BURY GARBAGE!

DISPOSING OF YOUR GARBAGE

Never bury garbage, but burn it on green sticks over a fire until consumed. This type of pit-cooking fire does the trick.

Wet garbage may be dried on hot stones heated in your fire.

When garbage is dry from hot stones, move to fire and burn.

AND SO TO BED

If the night is warm and clear you'll need no shelter at all other than your sleeping bag or blankets. Be sure there are no stones or small branches where you lay your sleeping gear; it's amazing how big a pebble can grow during the night, and how a twig becomes a log.

Have plenty of firewood handy for your fire, for nothing makes a camp site more cheerful than a good blazing fire and the knowledge that you can keep it going as long as you are awake. Have plenty of wood and then some more, for an all-night fire takes a lot, and no one likes to crawl out of a sleeping bag to go out and cut more. Have the fuel close enough so that you can add to the fire without getting up to do so. Use "lazy logs" and a shoving stick.

Be sure that you have emptied your pockets into a safe place or a paper bag, loosened your belt and anything else that is tight. Put all articles of wearing apparel under shelter from the morning dew, and have that flashlight handy at all times. Light your small lantern if you have one, or a sheltered candle light.

Protect your food by hanging in a tree out of reach of small visitors and insects and cover clean dishes with a pail or paper bag. Never go to bed without washing your cooking and eating utensils and picking up the camp area, for safety after dark and better sanitation.

Put all axes where they cannot be tripped over or fallen upon. This also applies to hand axes and hunting knives. Remove your knife, with its sheath, from your belt and keep with your flashlight within easy reach.

Before getting into bed be sure that your bed is protected from above and below with a waterproof cover, particularly from below, and that you have as many blankets under as over you. If it is a cold night, exercise violently for a few moments before getting into your bed so that your body will give off more heat to warm it up. Fleece-lined slippers will keep your feet warm if chilly.

"GOOD NIGHT CHECK LIST"

A—FOOD PROTECTED FROM ANIMALS AND INSECTS

B—ALL DISHES WASHED AND COVERED

C—"LAZY LOGS" TO FEED INTO FIRE

D—STICK TO PUSH "LAZY LOGS" WITH

E—FUEL CUT FOR BREAKFAST FIRE

F—KINDLING PROTECTED BY SHELTER

G—SHOES UNDER COVER FOR NIGHT

H—SMALL ARTICLES IN PAPER BAGS

I—FLASHLIGHT HANDY TO REACH

J—SMALL LANTERN TO BURN ALL NIGHT

CAMPING SAFETY

Cut all root loops about the camp area to prevent tripping. Watch out for rocks that tilt, and after a rain beware of slippery leaves.

Keep all axes protected when not in use, either set into a log end or between two. Paint orange visibility band on handle.

Never pitch camp below overhanging ledge for danger of falling rocks after rainstorm.

Break off all sharp branches about camp area to save jabbed face and eyes when walking about after dark.

CAMPING CAN BE FOOL PROOF, BUT NOT DARN FOOL PROOF!

A primary rule of safe camping or hiking is to be sure where you put your hands and feet. It's also a fine idea to look where you sit.

Never risk injury by putting your hands into tree openings, small caves or holes in the ground. You may be bitten or stung.

When putting down dishes or pans of hot liquids or food, be sure they will not slide or tip and cause burns.

Be ever alert to fire and sparks. If your tent should catch fire pull it down at once. A standing tent burns quickly but a down tent can be put out by stamping, wetting or beating.

37

FIRST AID IN CAMP

MOVE BROKEN OR SPRAINED LIMBS AS LITTLE AS POSSIBLE TO BANDAGE OR PUT IN SPLINT. DO NOT TRY TO SET. GET TO A DOCTOR AT ONCE.

If bone seems to be broken, make a splint out of bark slabs, sticks or anything handy. Pad with leaves, clothing or evergreen tips. If broken bone protrudes, DO NOT TOUCH IN ANY WAY, but if you have a sterile dressing protect bone end with it. Hurry to doctor!

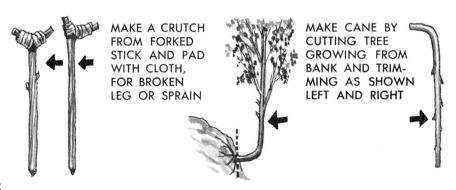

MAKE A CRUTCH FROM FORKED STICK AND PAD WITH CLOTH, FOR BROKEN LEG OR SPRAIN

MAKE CANE BY CUTTING TREE GROWING FROM BANK AND TRIMMING AS SHOWN LEFT AND RIGHT

38

Minor burns from a hot pan handle, etc., may be treated with burn ointment or a paste of baking soda and water. Do not open blisters. If skin is cracked or charred get to a doctor at once. Apply nothing greasy, or such things as cotton batting.

If cut is small, apply antiseptic dressing and bandage. If bleeding is severe apply sterile pad tightly to cut, and bandage. Apply tourniquet between cut and heart and release only under doctor's orders.

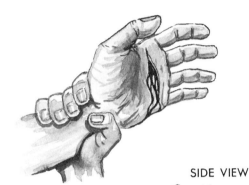

SIDE VIEW

BLACK WIDOW SPIDER

LUMP FROM NON-DEADLY INSECT

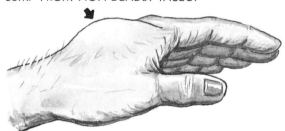

1/2"

UNDERSIDE

The bite of the Black Widow spider is serious. (Look for bright red hourglass on underside.) Apply tourniquet between bite and heart, cut into bite area and apply strong suction. Pack in ice if at all possible. Same treatment for snake bite. Get to doctor!

SUCTION HERE

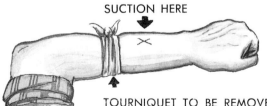

TOURNIQUET TO BE REMOVED BY DOCTOR

CAMPING DUDS

The main thing in camping gear is comfort and protection from the kind of weather you will encounter. Wear clothes you won't worry about no matter what happens. They should be strong and rugged.

FOR CAMP

Shoes should be comfortable, in good repair and waterproof. Take slippers for wear about camp.

GOOD CAMPING SHOE DESIGN

WINTER

SNAKE COUNTRY

Moccasin-toed shoes are particularly comfortable. Wear shoes with good ankle-supporting height. High boots in snake country and rubber bottoms in damp areas.

SUMMER

FOR SLEEPING

WINTER

An old felt hat is fine for camping; protects face, sheds water and can be used as pail. Ski cap good for winter. Knitted toque is fine for sleeping either winter or summer. Take extra socks and shoelaces.

Any kind of rugged comfortable pants will do; khaki, blue jeans, or woolen, depending upon the weather. A good kind for all-around camping has rubber-lined knees and seat and knitted anklets to go inside boots and keep out cold and insects. Wear pants with wide belt loops, plenty of pockets and in good repair.

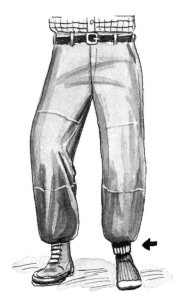

Shirts should be bright for safety, warm, and with two pockets. Take an extra flannel shirt for cool days.

A pull-over sweater will feel good at night if cool.

A water-repellent outer jacket that is windproof should be taken along. This with extra shirt and sweater will keep you really warm.

41

SO YOU'RE LOST!

The first thing to do when you realize that you are lost is to sit down! This helps prevent panic and also keeps you from becoming further lost. Don't worry about food for you can go a week without it if you save your strength and have plenty of water. Save any food you have with you as long as possible, and eat it sparingly. Try and backtrack to camp but if you can't, use your compass to keep going straight.

To prevent becoming lost, in strange country, note landmarks as you move about camping area. Blaze trees as you explore and let others know about where you are going to go, and then stick to plan. Carry food with you, a compass, waterproof matches, and some common sense.

SET WATCH FOR STANDARD TIME!

If you have no compass but a watch that is fairly accurate, that will do almost as well, if the sun is out. Set a little twig on the face as shown so that shadow runs down hour hand. South is halfway to noon (forward) in the morning, and halfway to noon (backward) in the afternoon.

42

SIGNALS FOR HELP

SMUDGE BY DAY

Find a high point of land or a big clearing and build a fire. On this heap green leaves, ferns, and bushes. The dense smoke may bring you help from friends or fire wardens looking for fires.

BRIGHT FIRE BY NIGHT

At night build a big fire to let folks know where you are, keep you busy and warm. Build a shelter and relax. Don't try to travel at night no matter how desperate you may be.

GUNSHOTS AT NIGHT

Gunshots during the day, if the hunting season is on, may be of little help. Shots at night may bring game wardens, looking for poachers, to rescue you. Three shots a minute apart spell SOS to woodsmen, but wait a half hour between the three shot groups to bring help.

43

FINDING YOUR WAY

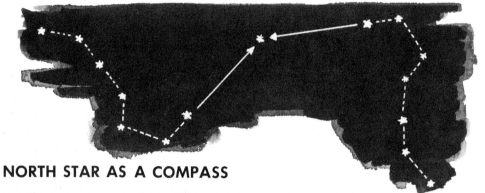

NORTH STAR AS A COMPASS

Finding the North Star (Polaris) is simple. Find the Big Dipper and then sight along the line of the two stars forming the side away from the handle. The first bright star you come across is the North Star. No matter what time of year or what position the Dipper is in, these two stars point to Polaris, almost exactly true north.

If you are lost in strange country and can see no familiar landmarks, climb a tree to get above the foliage and look for an outstanding point: mountain, lake, or deep valley. From this high perch you may also spot smoke, a ranger tower or other point to head for. If you see a good-sized stream, head for it and follow it downstream to civilization. This will keep you supplied with fresh water and possibly game, as well as leading you to larger rivers and eventually signs of man. Small streams may lead you to an uninhabited lake or swamp but that chance must be taken if the situation is serious. If near an outstanding mountain, head for the top where you may find a trail to lead you to help. Go slowly, save your strength.

CAMPING TIPS

If the camping trip is to be for only a day or so, take paper plates, spoons and forks (you'll have your hunting knife) to save time washing dishes. The plates and other utensils can be burned in fire.

A hank of "clothesline" often comes in handy in many ways, pitching tents, making shelters, hanging clothes, etc.

A few nails and a coil of copper wire are handy.

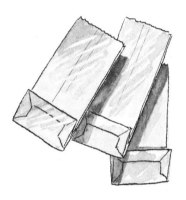

A half-dozen paper bags are handy for left-over food, pocket contents while sleeping, covering opened cans, and starting fires.

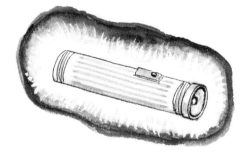

A luminous flashlight will save you hunting in the dark for a lost light. Take a flashlight for every man.

Waterproof your matches by dipping them in melted wax before leaving home. Take along a couple of the so-called "plumber's" or "watch-light" candles for night lights and helping to start damp wood for your fire.

MORE CAMPING TIPS

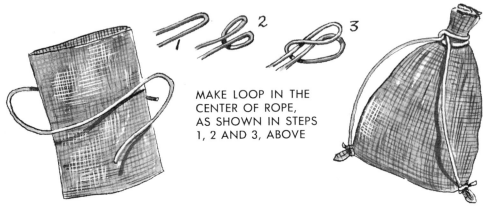

MAKE LOOP IN THE CENTER OF ROPE, AS SHOWN IN STEPS 1, 2 AND 3, ABOVE

If you do not happen to have a regular knapsack, or need an extra one, use a burlap or canvas bag and a length of rope. Make a loop, as shown above, over bag's neck and tie rope ends to sack corners.

Emergency candle holder can be made as shown from jackknife.

Don't risk a burn from hot pan or pail handles; use holder or bunch of leaves unless sure it is cool.

Rub garbage off plates with leaves and use notched stick to hold over fire to sterilize.

Before putting pot over fire, rub with pasty soap for easier cleaning later. Soot does not stick.

Use forked stick to hold pot or pail cover on and keep handle cool.

If hornets pester you, try hanging a skinned trout over some water nearby. They will attack it, gorge themselves and fall off into water to drown.

Protect lenses of compass and flashlight with pieces of Scotch tape. If broken, glass will be held in place by tape.

Damp shoes should be dried slowly away from fire. Fill with warm dry pebbles to help the process inside.

47

GIVE WILDLIFE A...

BREAK

Remember – Only you can
PREVENT FOREST FIRES!

...HEED IT!